THE HIGHER ED MARKETING COMMUNICATIONS ASSESSMENT

Evaluate Your Progress, Identify Opportunities
and Take Action!

KEVIN ANSELMO

TABLE OF CONTENTS

INTRODUCTION

Devising and executing a marketing communications strategy is no easy task. You probably understand this well if you are in either of the following positions:

- Dean of a school

- Director of a center, group or unit

- Leader of a marketing communications team

- Manager of a function within a marketing communications team

- Young professional aspiring to take on more leadership in marketing communications

All too often, individuals within a marketing communications team are off working in siloes, doing their own thing. There isn't clarity around big picture goals. PR professionals are generating media visibility that isn't tied to any strategy. Content is being created just for the sake of it. Ditto for social media and other online marketing tactics.

There are many drawbacks to working in such a disjointed way. You leave many benefits on the table in terms of advancing your organization forward. Even worse, it is difficult for a team to respond appropriately to the change and disruption in the industry, potentially leading to negative outcomes for different stakeholders. Individuals operating in siloes can end up competing with their own colleagues, as opposed to working together as a part of a team. This can obviously be detrimental for morale and engagement. Resources – both human and financial – are wasted.

Imagine the opposite: a marketing communications team in which all colleagues are clear on key messages and common goals and are working together to address them through their different functional expertise. Market conditions and the ever-changing communications landscape necessitate working in such a way.

"Schools need to develop a value proposition that not only resonates with their stakeholders (students, faculty, employers, the professions, government) but also clearly articulates what makes them different and why that distinction is relevant to the market," wrote Mark Farrell, a professor at RMIT University, and John Davis, an Executive Director with Duke Corporate Education, in an article for EFMD's Global Focus Magazine (the two are authors of the book *The Market Oriented University - Transforming Higher Education*).

Farrell and Davis' charge is easy to say, but difficult to execute. Strategies and structures need to be in place for optimal marketing communications integration. It is an ongoing process and requires constant evaluation. On that note, the following book takes you through a series of 10 yes/no questions to assess different aspects of your marketing communications operations. Following each question are a short explanation and steps to consider in addressing each particular area. The analysis is based on my:

- previous experiences working full-time for two top business schools (Duke University's Fuqua School of Business and IMD in Switzerland)
- work with different clients since starting my consulting business in 2013
- interviews I have conducted with experts
- observations on some of the best practice in the field

We need to take the time to assess our strategies and processes. In this spirit, I encourage you to carefully consider each question. It is my hope that such an evaluation will serve as a springboard for you to take your school or organization's marketing communications operations to the next level! Let's get started.

1

DO YOU HAVE INTERNAL CLARITY ABOUT WHAT YOU DO – BOTH FROM AN INSTITUTIONAL AND DEPARTMENTAL LEVEL?

There is a proverb that goes "where there is no vision, the people perish." This is certainly true for institutions and teams.

At the institutional level, consider if the majority of your employees are crystal clear about what your school or program is all about? Would they be able to state the essence of your value propositions to different external audiences?

From a departmental level, is there clarity around the goals for your marketing communications operations? Do the members of your team buy in to what you are trying to achieve? Do other departments within your institution understand, in principle, your key marketing communications goals? If there is lack of alignment internally, then it obviously makes external understanding more difficult.

Another dimension to internal clarity relates to employee disengagement. According to *Gallup's State of the Global Workplace* report, only 13% of employees worldwide are engaged at work. Gallup estimates that roughly $450 billion is lost due to disengagement. Internal clarity isn't the end all solution to resolving this engagement quandary. However, when you consider that we spend the majority of our waking hours at work, it certainly is a useful to understand what we are all working towards both institutionally and within our different teams.

You need to have internal buy-in about your institution or organization's key mission, vision and values. This might mean clarifying it for the first time, or modifying what is currently in place. It is easy to write that you need to "get internal buy-in". It is an arduous task to execute on this given that many different key groups and players are involved.

If you haven't done so already, I suggest that you create a message map. At the core, identify a few key words that describe what your institution or group does. Then think through and define the related 3-5 key messages. Under each of those messages, then come up with the different proof points and examples that demonstrate how you live out these messages. Type "University of Missouri Extension's message map" in Google to see a great example of this.

There are many different ways to define/re-evaluate your mission, vision, values and key messages. Here is one pathway that you may want to consider:

1. Interview internal and external stakeholders to hear their perspectives. You don't want to craft messaging solely based on your perspective. Sure, the leader and team can have in mind some of this language, but you want to be certain this is aligned with the reality, and also that you are bringing others along in the process. So identify a group of internal and external stakeholders and craft a series of interview questionnaires for each group. Summarize each of these interviews within one document.

2. Assess others. This is not about examining competitors and copying their language, but rather to see how different groups communicate their value propositions. I would suggest evaluating both traditional competitors as well as groups that are a bit outside of the box to what your school or organization does. For example, when leading this process for a business school, my client and I were able to glean great insights and inspiration by evaluating IDEO, a design consultancy that is innovative both in its work as well as its communications. Again, summarize the findings onto to this master document that also includes the interviews from the step above.

3. Identify themes to inform key messaging strategy. Now that you have this document with the summaries, you should be able to capture interesting themes and ideas. Note the different keywords, trends and communications tactics that continually stand out.

4. Draft content and message map. You need to put pen to paper. I would suggest first coming up with the message map. From there, you can craft a mission, vision and values. Look at this as an initial draft that serves as a springboard for reaction and further discussion.

5. Share for feedback. Consider presenting to different small groups for discussion.

6. Revise and align. Based on the feedback, revise accordingly, and get buy-in across the leadership team. You then want to think about training stakeholders about how to integrate new messaging into their roles, cascading throughout all communications collateral, disseminating via the complete communications mix and measuring accordingly, topics that we explore in the next chapter.

From a team point of view, you can go with a more scaled back version of the six-step process outlined above. Different leaders will surely approach this according to their own respective styles. But in principle aligning the team around what you do, why you do it and the values you will live by – and then reinforcing this on a regular basis – goes a long way to establishing a compass to guide your different activities.

2

IS YOUR KEY MESSAGING CASCADED ON YOUR DIFFERENT MARKETING COMMUNICATIONS COLLATERAL? IS IT PRESENTED FROM AN EXTERNAL POINT OF VIEW?

In answer to the first part of this question, if your mission statement is buried somewhere on your computer and nobody else knows about it, then the answer is "no".

In regard to the second part of this question, I keep in mind a metaphor I heard from communications expert Gini Dietrich. She advised in her book *Spin Sucks* to consider whether you are speaking French in your communications. By that, are you always talking about "we, we, we" (oui, oui, oui) in your messaging? I don't know about you, but I don't necessarily enjoy the company of people who just want to talk about themselves. I prefer the company of people who find connections between what they do and myself. Hence, don't just communicate "we do this," and "we do that". Make sure to communicate the "you" – your targeted audience.

Below are different ways you can consider cascading your key messaging, crafted from an external point of view (non French). Note that we delve into some of these tactics in more detail in other chapters.

- **Institutional website pages**. This may consist of your home page, About Us section and perhaps special sections dedicated to the key message topics. Do an inventory of how often you use the word "we" as opposed to "you" to ensure you are communicating from an external perspective.
- **Brochures**. If you have brochures for a number of programs, consider integrating some short and sweet boilerplate language, potentially adapted to the context of the program.
- **Messaging points for deans and senior leaders who interact with media**. Prepare a document for senior leadership, highlighting links between the interview subject and the key messages. Incorporate sound bites and find newsworthy hooks related to the messages.
- **Speeches or presentations by senior leadership**. Perhaps this might mean having a standard slide that highlights some of your key messaging and can be incorporated into any type of presentation. You could also think about preparing a standard presentation that can be used by leaders when talking about the school or program.
- **Social media bios**. This is ideal real estate to highlight your key messaging.
- **Institutional videos**. You could think about doing a short video that explains your school or program's messages in a visually compelling way.
- **Email marketing**. Key to your email marketing is to provide educational and useful content that resonates with a targeted audience. Within this guideline, you can integrate your key messages through standard features (i.e. – including a tagline for example, or integrating a link in all campaigns that shows an institutional video that highlights key messaging).
- **Content marketing**. As you think about creating relevant and educational content for specific targeted audiences, think about how you can incorporate key messaging. For example, if you do an interview podcast, you can have intro and outro language that incorporates key messaging. You can also think about cascading content by fleshing out thought leadership

around some of your key messages. So for example, if your school has a key message of global leadership, you can think creating special content around this theme (i.e. – a podcast series called Global Leadership).

- **SEO**. Related to content marketing, think about how you can integrate keywords associated with your messaging in your content and throughout your online materials.
- **Alumni relations**. Part of this may entail in-person updates to keep this key constituency abreast about your new developments at the school and integrating messaging into this discussion. It might also take the form of a regular newsletter or update crafted specifically for this group.
- **Internal communications from top leadership that reinforces key messages**. There are various ways to approach this, from written communication to in-person events, among other ways. Key is to create some mechanism in which leadership regularly updates the community about priorities and developments.
- **Mobilizing colleagues**. The cascade process starts by training your colleagues on how to use the key messaging in their respective roles. You don't want your colleagues to take your key messages and recite them back sounding like a bunch of robots. But you do want your colleagues all essentially "singing from the same hymn sheet", though adapting the key messaging as it relates to their different responsibilities. They can then potentially integrate aspects of the key messaging into their personal communications.
- **Measure**. If you are serious about the cascade, think through the metrics to measure success. It could entail periodical surveys, anecdotal feedback, keyword analysis and progress towards achieving the big picture goals reflected in the messaging.

3

DO YOU HAVE AN EDITORIAL MISSION TO GUIDE YOUR CONTENT MARKETING EFFORTS?

If you are answered "no", and if your school or program is either creating content inconsistently or not seeing the desired impact from your content marketing efforts, then you should consider crafting an editorial mission statement to provide clarity for you, your colleagues and potentially your external audiences.

The radical changes in the digital communications infrastructure have made it possible for any organization or individual to be a media company. To a certain extent, institutional YouTube channels, blogs and podcasts compete for individuals' attention just as TV stations, radio stations and newspapers do. The problem is that many institutional content hubs are inconsistent (for example, a blog updated every six months) and/or the content is not addressing a particular issue that resonates with your targeted audience (for example, content that reads like a brochure copy and is focused on a school or program's features). Content marketing is not about selling, but rather educating and informing. Author and speaker David Meerman Scott summarizes this quite succinctly when he says "Educate and inform instead of interrupt and sell."

Most of us raise our defenses when we feel that we are being sold to. By providing educational and informative content that doesn't overtly sell, you can overcome this barrier. You maintain attention and cut through the clutter of all the sales noise that is out there. The content is more likely to be shared via social media or found via search. Not many of us find brochure links shared in our Facebook feeds! On the other hand, content that addresses a particular issue and in some way makes our lives better is more likely to be shared. When your brand creates this type of content, it becomes the trusted source. We ultimately do business with those that we know, like and trust.

If you want to be serious about your content creation and reap some of the related benefits, consider modeling some of the traditional media's approaches.

Editorial mission

It starts by defining an editorial mission. Most every media outlet has an editorial mission that answers three questions:

- Who is the core audience?
- What will you deliver to them?
- What is the desired outcome?

As an example of an individual editorial mission statement, consider *Marketing Magazine* in Canada:

Marketing is Canada's definitive source for news, analysis and insights into the business of marketing. We help marketers by delivering what they need to win in today's fast-changing industry – on our digital and video platforms, in Marketing magazine and at our industry-leading awards and events. Our mission is to engage, inspire and inform with great storytelling that makes sense of disruption and change.

Our key audience is made up of the industry's top marketers and the major decision-makers when it comes to setting strategy and spending decisions. Marketing is the go-to news brand for influencers at creative, media and PR agencies, as well as the broader marketing community in social media, digital, publishing and ad tech.

Stanford University's Graduate School of Business personifies an editorial mission by stating:

Stanford Business publications are dedicated to sharing management research and insights from the global community of experts and leaders affiliated with Stanford Graduate School of Business.

We publish Stanford Business magazine, the free Stanford Business email newsletter, and here at our digital home. We also publish through media syndication agreements with some of the world's best-known publications and our YouTube channel.

Our goal is to provide current and aspiring leaders with the information and ideas they need to help them change lives, organizations, and the world.

I encourage you to answer and apply these editorial mission questions for yourself. It will help you be strategic and focused.

Editorial beats

Most media outlets have editorial beats. For instance, a newspaper will have someone covering the police beat, the education beat, the sports beat, etc. As part of your institutional content marketing initiatives, you may also want to consider adapting editorial beats in the same way. You may want to refer to your message map and link content themes to key messages.

Let's say that you are a School of Public Policy. You want your school to be known for a specialized degree that focuses on refugee resettlement. Your editorial mission is focused on providing prospective students with the reason to study refugee resettlement and sharing the latest analysis of this topic with alumni and policy makers.

Let's say within this broad category, you define three editorial beats: 1) best practice; 2) research; and 3) community perspectives.

Ideas for titles and subjects for the best practice beat would be:

- How refugees can best learn a new language
- How refugees can secure meaningful employment
- How religious organizations can integrate refugees into their congregations
- Other how-to best practice

For the research beat, titles and subjects could be:

- Resources overview
- How to teach students to be responsible researchers and policy makers as it relates to refugee adaptation
- Case studies
- Analysis of research on refugee adaptation

For the community perspectives ideas, this could be an opportune time to make your audiences the story. This could involve:

- Interviews with refugees
- Interviews with alumni who work in this particular space
- Interviews with NGO leaders working in this space
- Guest contributions from your community

From each category, you could easily flesh out additional topics.

Similarly, I encourage you to think about your big picture key objectives and priorities. Come up with content themes (beats) and then the related titles.

Editorial calendar

It is important to think about the driving forces that will enable you to execute your content goals. There is a big difference between creating content based on inspiration vs. an obligation to achieve a goal. Your favorite news anchor doesn't create content based on whether or not he or she "feels" like it on a particular day. Inspiration will only take you so far. If you feel like creating a piece of content, you will do so at your convenience. If you have a responsibility to create a piece of content, then you will do so regardless of circumstances.

An editorial calendar can serve as a tool to help execute on your content goals. Most traditional media outlets use an editorial calendar. The editorial calendar can outline the subject, description and deadlines for a particular piece of content. Maybe the goal is that each month, you will create one new piece of content across your three editorial beats, ensuring three new pieces each month and 36 for the year. The deliverables may vary, but consistency is key. On the next pages is a template that you can consider adapting and integrating for your institution or group.

TYPE	RELATED BEAT	DETAILS	DEADLINE
January			
February			
March			
April			
May			
June			

TYPE	RELATED BEAT	DETAILS	DEADLINE
July			
August			
September			
October			
November			
December			

4

DO YOU HAVE A COMPELLING "LEAD MAGNET" TO HELP YOU GENERATE NEW LEADS?

For starters, let me clarify the definition of a lead magnet. A lead magnet is offering a compelling piece of content to a particular audience in exchange for an email sign-up. This is not about buying lists, but rather earning email subscribers on your own. This is also a bit more nuanced than requiring prospects to provide their email address in exchange for a brochure. Technically, this is a way of capturing emails that you can then market to in the future. But in my opinion, this tactic is a bit like proposing marriage during a first date.

I am guessing that 99% of you don't have a lead magnet. The reason I am quite sure about this is because I spent time researching this for a particular presentation and struggled to find compelling examples.

One great example of an effective lead magnet within higher education is IMD's Global Leader Index. (IMD is a business school in Switzerland and my former employer). The Global Leader Index is a survey in which individuals sign up and answer a series of questions. At the completion of the survey, respondents can see how their leadership skills compare to others. The school is able to then send the respondents information tailored to their interests and needs as part of its ongoing email marketing.

James Henderson, a professor at IMD and a member of the management team responsible for programs and innovation, shared some insights on this topic when I interviewed him on my podcast.

"Most universities and business schools provide information on their website, and then provide dates and then 'click download brochure'," he said. "You don't know much about those people and can't provide much information. You end up providing generic information about the school that might be considered spam for the prospect. With this Global Leader Index, people provide information and in return they get a result and then they receive fantastic follow-up because we know exactly where they stand."

Over 12,000 individuals have completed the survey. The school has used this survey to support various aspects of its sales, marketing and communications.

"Rather than creating push-based marketing, we are trying turn that on its head and creating more pull-based marketing," said Henderson. "We are still on this journey, but that is direction we are moving and I would suggest where other schools should be going."

Some of the best examples of using lead magnets to sell a course or program come from outside of traditional higher education. I started my own business at the end of 2013 and make it a point to regularly follow some of the best examples of small business owners who are particularly adept at leveraging online marketing tactics. Most all of those who are successful have compelling lead magnets in which they are providing a valuable piece of content in exchange for an email. Once that person is on the email list, they receive regular updates, both in the form of ongoing educational and useful information as well as the occasional sales message promoting a particular offering.

Consider how online course creator Michael Hyatt uses lead magnets. He actually has four different eBook lead magnets on his homepage, each of which address a pain point of a particular audience segment and ultimately link to his different programs. As a result, he is then able to provide more relevant content in his ongoing email marketing campaigns. For example, I subscribed to his lead magnet focused on leadership and then receive additional relevant content and occasional promotional offerings that relate to this subject. This follow-up messaging he sends me obviously differs from the lead magnets focused on other topics.

Ideal types of lead magnets to sell some sort of program, course or related service would be offering a free:

- **eBook**. See the above example from Michael Hyatt. In addition, this book was created to serve as a lead magnet for marketers and communicators working in the higher education space. I have a separate lead magnet for academics. Previously, I made the mistake of combining these audiences, and therefore crafting the ideal messaging that would resonate with both audiences was nearly impossible. I am now able to provide relevant content to each list and incorporate some of my different offerings targeted to these two different audiences.
- **Online course**. Chris Ducker is an online marketer who sells a membership site in which he provides new content each month to paid subscribers. He builds up his email list by offering a free online course that he calls "Launchpad". This lead magnet is prominently featured on his homepage.
- **Assessments or surveys**. Any content that gives users feedback about their performance makes for an interesting lead magnet. The example from IMD would fit into this category.
- **Tickets to attend a live event**. Many schools in the business education space offer an "MBA for a Day" type of event in which prospective students can experience case studies, meet faculty and students in person and generally get a feel for the school. To attend such an event, prospective students need to provide their email address.

- **Research**. Social Media Marketing World is an annual event held in San Diego, California that draws some 4,000 marketing professionals. The event is organized by the company behind the popular website, *South Media Examiner*. According to its website, Social Media Examiner has over 500,000 email subscribers at the time of this writing. Their lead magnet is its annual Social Media Marketing Industry Report. The language associated with the lead magnet is as follows: *Wondering how your peers are using social media? In our 8th annual social media study (56 pages, 90 charts) of 5000+ marketers, you'll discover which social networks marketers most plan on using more (hint: it's not what you think), how much time they spend on social media and much more! Get this free report and never miss another great article from Social Media Examiner.*

As you consider your messaging and audiences, think about creating related lead magnets. You want these lead magnets to be linked to your core objectives, but it is important that the lead magnet itself is valuable and useful content that addresses your audience's needs, and is not an overt sales pitch.

5

IS YOUR EMAIL MARKETING PROVIDING RELEVANT, USEFUL AND EDUCATIONAL CONTENT FOR SPECIFIC TARGETED AUDIENCES?

This builds on the Question 4 topic of lead magnets. Once you have individuals who have opted in, you have some background as to their interests. You can then provide content via email marketing that is pertinent to this particular audience segment.

Email marketing is a tactic to reach a big picture goal. Underpinning success in email marketing is an integrated marketing communications team. Since starting my own business, I have signed up for numerous newsletters coming from higher education, online entrepreneurs, think tanks and organizations. The following are some best practice tactics that I have identified. Perhaps these are tactics that you might want to consider integrating into your email marketing.

- **Subject lines.** One academic group I subscribe to sends out a regular newsletter with the most banal of subject lines. Basically each subject line states: "XYZ Organization News Digest - Week Ending 12/2". Another newsletter I subscribe to says "Student Newsletter November 2016". In the midst of our busy lives in which we all strive for clean inboxes, it would be far more effective to have a subject line that entices a specific individual to open and potentially click through. When you create a subject line, make sure you are not speaking in "French" and focusing on the "we, we, we" but rather put yourself in the shoes of an ideal audience member and craft your message accordingly. Try to find different unique aspects of your content and incorporate that into your subject line. If this is a new way of working, you may want to experiment by dividing up your list and using different subject lines and then seeing which is generating the highest open rates. This can help you find the voice that best resonates with your audience.

- **Links**. There may be some select cases in which a newsletter type of email with lots of links makes sense, but in principle I suggest fewer links and more focus on a small number of topics.

- **Calls to action**. It certainly makes sense to incorporate calls to action into your email marketing, such as signing up for a program or downloading a brochure. But you need to be judicious in how often you communicate calls to actions and when you do so. I once heard an expert point out the 90 – 10 rule: 90% of valuable, non sales related content for every 10% of calls to action with sales messages. You can think of this in terms of an email that has 90% content and then on the right rail there are embedded images with calls to action. If you are thinking of a series, you can envision a number of emails that are focused on education, and then move into a sales message with a later email. There are lots of schools of thought on this. The key point is that if you are overly "salesy", success is difficult.

- **Frequency**. Content Marketing Institute (CMI) hosts major events and conducts trainings in different parts of the world throughout the year. There are many aspects of their marketing communications which you could model for your school, center or organization. In terms of email marketing frequency, CMI has built up an extensive list through its various compelling lead magnets and then delivers fresh new content everyday at 10:10 am US EST. It is like a Swiss train in terms of its reliability! You may not have the means to send out new email communications on a daily or even weekly basis. But it is advisable to have some sort of natural and regular cadence. I find it annoying to receive nothing from an organization for months, but then multiple sales emails show up in my inbox over the period of one week.

- **Ask!** In thinking about the big picture, you want to link together your key objectives and your audience's needs through the content you create. The problem is that often we are creating content based on what we think our audience cares about. To some extent, we have to use our intuition. However, from time to time it might make sense to be more deliberate and systematic in making sure content is aligned to the audience's expectations. The best way to do this is to ask the audience. Many of the most successful online entrepreneurs routinely solicit feedback from their audiences. I encourage you do to the same, whether it be an online survey or doing a series of in-depth qualitative interviews with select individuals.

These are just a few areas that I wanted to highlight that can potentially serve as a springboard for you. You obviously want to evaluate other dimensions such as design, analytics, integrating social media, brand guidelines, etc.

6

IS YOUR SOCIAL MEDIA STRATEGIC?

For this question, I want to link back to Question 3 and your editorial mission. I would suggest that your social media reflect your editorial mission and editorial beats. Of course both these areas relate back to key messaging and big picture goals. Here is an example of how this might play out.

Themes

We begin by fleshing out the content themes. For example the themes and related beats for a particular school may be:

- Alumni: thought leadership from alumni, features and anecdotes.
- Programs: seminars, what is happening in the classroom, faculty in programs and pictures of slide presentations from class.
- Thought leadership: press articles, content marketing (article by a professor highlighted in email marketing), books, activities of the dean or director, etc.
- Location: news and pictures about the city and country where the school is located.
- Highlighting partners: chairs, clients, students and other school stakeholders.
- Turn back the clock: old pictures, history.

Frequency and Channels

Noting the importance of consistency, create editorial expectations for each beat and channel. For example, perhaps this might involve the following:

BEAT	Facebook	Twitter	Instagram	LinkedIn
Alumni	2 per week	2 per week	1 per week	1 per week
Programs	2 per week	2 per week	1 per week	1 per week
Thought Leadership	5 per week	5 per week	1 per week	5 per week
Location	1 per week	1 per week	1 every 2 weeks	1 every 2 weeks
Partners	2 per week	1 per week	1 every 2 weeks	1 every 2 weeks
History	1 per week	1 per week	1 every 2 weeks	1 every 2 weeks

Execution

Working within this framework, you should of course take into account that there are differences in how messages should be communicated across channels. Each network has its own unique way of "nuancing" the content so it is relevant and appropriate for the particular channel. In some cases, there are additional activities related to a particular network (i.e. - building community in a LinkedIn alumni group or leveraging a particular hashtag on Twitter during a school event). There are opportunities to integrate the occasional sales message appropriate for a particular channel, as well as the possibility to use promoted posts when it makes sense.

It is important to create a structure to operate within this context. For example, this could involve the following:

Editor in Chief: Individual who oversees the entire process and serves as the final gatekeeper of content before it is disseminated. This person also reviews metrics regularly and shares feedback with the team.

Reporter #1: Colleague responsible for creating thought leadership content and also manages Twitter.

Reporter #2: Colleague responsible for alumni related content and also manages LinkedIn.

Reporter #3: Colleague responsible for history content and also manages Instagram.

Reporter #4: Colleague responsible for partners and programs and also manages Facebook.

Process

Key to success is using a structure in which team members are held accountable and are part of a bigger picture. For this particular process, each "reporter" puts content suggestions for the upcoming week into a shared team folder by the close of business on a particular day (let's say Thursday for this example). On Fridays, the editor in chief reviews, edits and approves all social media content for that upcoming week. The managers of each account can then plan to disseminate the content for the upcoming week, either posting regularly or using a scheduling tool. On Mondays, the team meets to discuss the long-term editorial overview, review of the previous week (ideally incorporating analytics) and sharing of best practice, etc.

This process ensures regular content creation and a consistent voice from the brand. However, key to social media success is also acting and reacting in real-time: responding to questions directed to the brand, jumping on trending topics and engaging where necessary. It might make most sense for this responsibility to fall under the editor in chief, though each reporter can make suggestions when opportunities arise. At times, the editor in chief assigns a real-time activity to the appropriate reporter (i.e. – the Twitter reporter is responsible for attending an event and tweeting out quotes and pictures from the different speakers).

Tools to Support Process

- Google shared documents, which includes a tab for each beat and then columns with the suggested content and the approved post.
- Scheduling tools such as Tweetdeck, Hootsuite or Buffer.
- Content calendar for an integrated marketing communications operation.

Additional Short-Term Next Step Possibilities

- Update channel profile bios to reflect messaging.
- Promote social media channels in email signatures, business cards, brochures, print materials, presentation templates and email marketing.
- Provide necessary training for any "reporters".

Additional Long-Term Possibilities

- Train senior leadership to use social media on their own, with potential support from the marketing communications team.
- Train additional ambassadors – faculty, students and directors, among others.
- Invest in other mediums like SlideShare and SnapChat once success is achieved in the other identified channels.
- Consider using live streaming to showcase the school or program's experience.

7

IS YOUR MEDIA RELATIONS DIRECTLY SUPPORTING YOUR INTEGRATED MARKETING COMMUNICATIONS GOALS?

An integrated marketing communication team means everyone is working towards common goals, while deploying different tactics. Media relations is one of those tactics.

Measuring how press coverage relates to marketing communications goals is difficult. Many view Advertising Value Equivalency, a framework that measures the value of a media hit, as flawed. I recently heard a story of somone who saw more direct sales of a service by being a guest on a niche podcast than they did from a mention in *The New York Times*. Brand awareness certainly has value. At the same time, it is easy to fall in the trap of vanity metrics when we showcase press coverage just for the sake of it. The coverage isn't related to the messages we want to be known for, the markets we serve and the audiences we want to reach. The coverage might look pretty, but in reality the value is limited as it relates to organizational goals.

Let's imagine your school has defined one of its key objectives is to be known for its expertise on doing business in emerging markets. This topic directly relates to a new executive education program offering that is targeted particularly for managers coming from Brazil,

Russia, India and China, as well as professionals from the United States looking to work in these markets. Working in an integrated way, here are media tactics that can help support this goal.

- **Relationships**: Please don't rely on media lists and then send press releases to anyone remotely linked to the subject area. Journalists are frequently bombarded with pitches. I spoke to an editor from *Inside Higher Education* who told me he receives 500 pitches a day! Journalists are quick to complain about the quality of these pitches. These complaints usually center on receiving untargeted pitches with no news angle (i.e. - blasting a press release to numerous journalists all at one time, regardless if that pitch is pertinent to the media outlet). Often times, journalists feel that the relevant information is not included and that the pitch is too long.

  There is a reason we use the words "media relations". The "spray and pray" to as many people as you can put together on a list is certainly not personifying "the relations" part of media relations.

  We also need to re-evaluate the term journalist. It doesn't take an advanced degree in rocket science to understand that the media landscape has changed dramatically. Shrinking newsrooms are the norm. With this dynamic, we are seeing traditional media outlets fill the void by bringing on guest contributors (*Forbes.com* is one of many examples). In addition, there are now influencers – academics, practitioners and other experts – as well as different brands that have amassed huge followings through their different blogs, podcasts and YouTube channels. These different outlets sometimes have audiences bigger than traditional media outlets. Yet many in media relations don't consider pitching and building relationships with these influencers, and instead solely focus on the traditional journalist.

Cut through the clutter and expand your approach to media relations by focusing on niche relationships that link the messages, markets and audiences related to the big picture objective. Let's think this through using the case of positioning the Doing Business in Emerging Markets program that is targeted for managers from the US, Brazil, Russia, India and China. First, consider identifying 5-10 key journalists/influencers in each of the five countries and who cover the topic of business in emerging markets. Study their previous stories and gain an understanding about how they work with experts and the types of stories they create. Follow them on social media, both from the personal account of the media relations representative as well as the institutional channels.

Also look for ways to build relationships that don't necessarily involve pitching a story. Meet and greets with leadership and the media relations personnel is a great place to start if you happen to be in the same location. As your school is a content creator, there might be ways to integrate journalists and influencers into your content. For example, my former employer Duke University does a fantastic job of inviting journalists to speak on different panels with other experts. I recently read an interview on the Duke business school's blog that featured a Q and A interview with an influential editor from *Handelsblatt* newspaper in Germany. In this case, the journalist is being interviewed. As you build relationships, you can connect the dots between the stories you want to place and the journalists' different needs.

- **Map your editorial calendar to targeted journalists**. As covered in Question 3, your marketing communications department should be thinking like a media outlet with its content marketing. Therefore, media relations professionals should be aware weeks and ideally months in advance about the institutional content that is on the horizon. Many traditional media outlets make their editorial priorities and calendars public. Also, as a result of your relationship building efforts, you have some awareness about topics your targeted journalists are covering. I would suggest creating a shared document for internal use that outlines different targeted media outlets' special reports and editorial guidelines. It helps media relations professionals know about what is on the horizon related to potential pitches. In addition, it helps institutional content creators know about topics to be potentially covering that are more likely to gain traction with traditional media outlets.

- **Leverage existing assets**. In this hypothetical case, several colleagues are working towards positioning the Business in Emerging Markets program. So this might mean that your colleagues are also creating assets (potentially videos, blog posts, etc.) linked to the program. This is low hanging fruit that might be useful from a media relations perspective. So if a professor has written a post for your school's blog on how to do business in India, think about how you might be able to syndicate that content with different media in the respective markets. Or maybe that particular thought leadership piece could lead to an interview with the journalists you have targeted.

- **Strategically promote media coverage**. Good news – you have secured excellent coverage related to the topic. Bad news – if you stop there, you aren't maximizing the impact. After you secure coverage, think integrated! Make sure that the coverage is disseminated on the school's different social media channels. Share this with your internal audiences, particularly thinking about how your community can be your "ambassador" and share it with their communities (we delve into this topic in more detail with Question 9). Think about displaying the press coverage on a nice PDF that can be used by your admissions/sales team to share with prospects. Integrate it into your alumni relations and email marketing. In other words, connect all the dots!

- **Integrate into online pressroom**. A great way to be of service to the media is by allowing them to find information quickly and easily via an online pressroom. This dedicated space on your site should include all the basics: downloadable images, bios of spokespeople, contact information, general guidelines, etc. It might also make sense to highlight different areas of expertise in which your organization can provide analysis. So for this example, you might want to consider having a section showcasing your experts on doing business in emerging markets. If you can incorporate the right keywords into your online pressroom, this could also help from an SEO perspective, just one more example of the value of media relations not necessarily linking directly to press coverage.

- **Try incorporating unique links**. We have already covered the challenge of measuring media output. The above tactics all play a role in supporting objectives. The most powerful way is to actually demonstrate a link between media coverage and incoming traffic to the website's program page. So for example, let's say you secure coverage in the form of a professor writing a guest contribution for a media outlet on doing business in emerging markets. As a final call to action, include a unique URL that goes to the program page. In your Google analytics, you are able to then see the number of individuals who clicked on the link and took particular actions as part of the sales process.

8

ARE ALUMNI INTEGRATED INTO YOUR MARKETING COMMUNICATIONS?

Let's work from the assumption that graduates had a positive experience with your school. If that's the case, then not integrating your alumni into your integrated marketing communications is a missed opportunity.

Some of the previous questions covered alumni in bits and pieces. I thought it was important to focus on the role of alumni as part of an integrated marketing communications operation in a stand-alone question. So let's evaluate opportunities to incorporate alumni leveraging earned media (traditional media relations), shared media (social media), owned media (content you own on your own hub) and paid media (advertising). Let's also assume that the big picture objective is the same as in Question 7: demonstrate thought leadership in the area of Doing Business in Emerging Markets (this particular program could be a good fit for the school's alumni).

- **Owned media**. Instead of the typical alumni feature that is more of a general feel good story, consider tying this to the main objective. So therefore, the feature would center around XYZ graduate's expertise on doing business in emerging markets. Or how about conducting an alumni survey with questions focused on doing business in emerging markets (perhaps you would have to segment your list in this scenario). Have the alumni share their expertise in the survey and then produce a white paper or some sort of research study that highlights trends and best practice. This white paper could serve as a lead magnet for prospects. Most poignantly, you have the opportunity for alumni to promote the white paper/research with their network. Asking alumni to promote general school content is one thing and certainly should be explored. But when you ask alumni to promote content that they are highlighted in, you will certainly get a higher return of individuals taking action.

You can also think about creating special programming – say a closed webinar from an expert on the topic – with your alumni community. The goal would be to encourage them to sign up for the program or recommend it to a colleague. Of course your regular alumni communications activities (i.e. – email marketing, events, etc.) should also incorporate the desired messages related to the key objective.

- **Shared media**. You are probably already connected to or are following your alumni on social media channels. Another dimension of this is the community aspect. Closed LinkedIn groups and Facebook communities are ideal platforms for such exchanges. Think about how you can incorporate your key objectives – in this case the doing business in the emerging markets theme – into these communities by fostering conversation and exchange around the topic.

- **Earned media**. We covered the aspect of communicating press coverage to stakeholders in Question 7. Building on that thought, consider pitching your alumni for potential media interviews on the topic of doing business in emeging markets. It is also worth tapping into your alumni network to identify any journalists who are alumni of your school. It may be a conflict of interest for them to particularly write about your school and the particular content theme you are pitching, but at a minimum they may be likely to connect you to their colleagues within the media outlet.

- **Paid media**. Sponsored content and paying to promote posts on social media can potentially be a good investment. The opportunities to segment audiences and be very targeted with paid posts ensure that your advertising investment is directed at the right audience. So you may want to promote posts to alumni around this particular key objective (i.e. – promoting survey and/or finished white paper) as another touch point.

DO YOU HAVE AN AMBASSADOR PROGRAM IN PLACE THAT ENCOURAGES YOUR COLLEAGUES TO DISSEMINATE CONTENT TO THEIR DIFFERENT AUDIENCES?

Training and mobilizing your colleagues to be communications ambassadors for your organization is the most efficient, economic and effective means to generate impact!

Your marketing communications department can be excellent as a stand alone team. You may have a brilliant strategy in place. You can have the right connections and craft really compelling stories. But you represent just one megaphone! Imagine what happens when you have "ambassadors" – your colleagues – who are out there effectively communicating their thought leadership, ideas and the organization's messages on their own. They develop their relationships, stories and followings on their own, amplifying your organization's message and connecting it to big picture organizational goals. Suddenly you have numerous megaphones communicating messages to different audiences.

The reality is that the public trusts your ambassadors. Edelman, the global public relations firm, has been surveying public trust levels for the past 16 years through the Edelman Trust Barometer. Their annual survey is released in January – 33,000 people in 27 global markets took part in the most recent survey. Academics consistently rank among the top as trusted sources (64 ranking). Also ranking high are technical experts (67 ranking). In comparison, CEOs' score is 49 and government officials a paltry 35.

For me there are two dimensions to ambassador training:

1) Equipping your colleagues with the communications skills so they can communicate their research and expertise effectively on their own to different audiences.

2) Mobilizing your colleagues to help communicate key institutional messages to their respective audiences. So this might mean colleagues sharing institutional announcements about a school initiative to their own community.

Ideally, you want to encompass both of these areas for your faculty and experts. There will probably more emphasis on the second component for administrative level employees.

Here are among the benefits of an ambassador program:

- Personifying "social business" – individuals throughout the organization strategically leveraging different channels to communicate key brand messages.
- Increased brand visibility – both for the organization and individuals.
- Amplification of brand messages.
- Mitigating risk of a communications crisis.
- Expansion of networks.
- Internal alignment.

On my podcast, I conducted separate interviews with Shel Holtz, a communications consultant, and Deborah Maue, VP of Marketing and Communications at Columbia College in Chicago, on the topic of ambassador programs. Based on their insights and some of my own experiences, here are some steps to keep in mind if you are looking to roll out an ambassador program for the first time.

- **Think about key objectives**. You can go in a number of different directions, but you have to be deliberate. What messages do you want your ambassadors to help you amplify? Is it related to one of your key messages? Is it related to a particular initiative? Your ambassadors will ideally follow your lead.
- **Leadership buy-in**. At a minimum, you want to have leadership on board with the goals of the ambassador program. Ideally, you want them to actually participate!
- **Start small**. Especially if you are doing this for the first time, think about getting a small group involved, test out to see what works, and then potentially expand the number of your ambassadors. Important to note that an ambassador program probably won't work well if it is forced. It should be voluntary, though do consider using different incentives to encourage participation.
- **Training**. This should be the cornerstone of an ambassador program. Outline the goals and provide the necessary education for your colleagues to execute. It certainly doesn't hurt to make the training fun as well!
- **Identify communications mechanisms**. How will your ambassadors receive information that they can consider sharing with their networks? A private Facebook group, newsletter or regular email could all be possibilities.
- **Ongoing support**. Many initiatives have a clear start and end date. For ambassador training, you ideally want this to be ongoing. Key will be to maintain momentum so it doesn't sputter out. So consider mechanisms such as contests, special events and add-on training as a means to motivate your ambassadors.

10

DO YOU HAVE THE PROCESSES, TOOLS AND STRUCTURES IN PLACE TO SUPPORT AN INTEGRATED MARKETING COMMUNICATIONS OPERATION?

This question is intentionally the last. Hopefully you can see the common thread of core business objectives linked between the nine previous questions. As you can probably imagine, it is impossible to optimally work in an integrated fashion if the answer to Question 10 is "no". If you feel that is the case for your team, or there are opportunities for improvement, here are some different processes, tools and structures that you can consider putting in place.

- **Performance reviews**. Raise your hand if you like performance reviews, either as the manager administering it or the employee being reviewed. I don't see many hands up. I despised performance reviews when I worked in organizations that used them. It felt bureaucratic. The questions were too broad and covered too much time. Professor David Burkus' brilliant book *Under New Management* highlights the flaws of traditional annual reviews and why more ongoing, regular feedback – done both formally and informally – is optimal.

This is particularly true among millennials. A Gallup survey found that millennial workers are more engaged than non-millennials when their managers provide frequent and consistent communication and feedback. Forty-four percent of millennials who report that their manager holds regular meetings with them are engaged, contrasting sharply with the 20% of engaged millennials who do not agree that their manager meets with them regularly. Gallup found that only 21% of millennials and 18% of non-millennials meet with their manager on a weekly basis.

It can be difficult to change course in performance reviews, as often these are HR policies put in place decades ago. Still, I would suggest trying to incorporate big picture goals into reviews. Also explore ways in which leaders are providing more regular feedback with employees.

- **Team meetings**. Do you meet regularly with the appropriate individuals who have an ongoing stake in your different marketing communications goals? If you do meet regularly, are these meetings centered on big picture goals? You and I both are not fans of meetings just for the sake of it. All too often, team meetings can feel like "fluff" in which individuals go around in a circle and update about their different activities. This type of meeting feels very tactic heavy, and not orientated towards big picture goals. So first make sure the right people are in the room. I encourage you to focus these meetings on the big picture goals you are looking to achieve and then have the different colleagues share their activities through this lens.

- **Online collaboration tools**. Consider leveraging tools that encourage conversation around goals. For example, with the online collaboation tool "Slack" you can set up channels for each of your big picture goals. From there, colleagues can dialogue around these channels and share the tactics they are using to achieve the different goals, thus providing a constant medium for conversation. Google docs can be useful for sharing team organizational documents, such as an editorial calendar. You should consider using some sort of medium to house key team documents, strategies and other related materials.

- **Measurement and reporting**. Are you and your colleagues clear about where website traffic is coming from, the success of different campaigns and other insights that can be gleaned from Google analytics? If not, think about putting in place a structure for all stakeholders on the team to be aware of this data, whether that is as part of in-person meetings or online conversation.

- **Media monitoring**. Do your colleagues have access to the tools that let them see how the school, competitors and related keywords are being communicated in both the traditional press as well as social channels? Think about using some sort of media monitoring service, and then consider who should be able to access it and how to report out key findings, both within the marketing communications team as well as other outside groups.

- **Learning**. Technological advances are constantly impacting marketing communications. It is imperative that we have our pulses on the latest news and trends so we can adapt accordingly. I believe one of the most important values to instill within marketing communications teams is the value of ongoing shared learning. There are entire books written on this subject, but as a summary some items to consider would be attending offsite conferences, organizing regular learning lunches (i.e. a weekly lunch gathering to watch an online course on a particular topic) and setting up channels with online collaboration tools like Slack which allow colleagues to share interesting things they learned.

NEXT STEPS

I truly hope that this book has been useful for you and that you have some new ideas on how to improve your marketing communications. I would love to hear your feedback as well as some of your ideas about areas I should address in update versions of this book. Please do let me know. My email is kevin@experientialcommunications.com or I can be reached on +1-919-260-0035.

Perhaps you are in one of following two categories:

1. You like the ideas in this book, and want to take action using your internal resources.

Fantastic. Take action! I would be keen to hear about your successes on how you and your colleagues have been able to use some of the ideas in this book to bring about positive change for your department and organization as a whole. Also, I would be really appreciative if you would share this book with your colleagues who might be able to benefit. Please direct them to www.experientialcommunications.com where they can sign up to receive this book free of charge.

2. There are lots ideas here that you would like to take action on, but you don't really know where to begin. You don't feel that you have the internal resources and you could benefit from an outside perspective.

I actually know someone who can help you and is available for hire! :)

I started my company Experiential Communications to help clients address many of the questions in this book. In a nutshell, we help institutions and groups develop and execute strategic marketing communications plans. Media training is another core component of our business.

I would be pleased to arrange an initial phone or Skype call with you to learn more about your marketing communications. Based on that discussion, we can explore whether it makes sense to work together. Email me at kevin@experientialcommunications.com to set up this call.

Here are how others describe the impact of our work in devising and executing marketing communications strategies:

"Kevin Anselmo of Experiential Communications has helped us as a staff, overseen largely by a group of university faculty, to navigate this space between academia and contracting and set us on a course to develop a more sustainable business model that will allow us to keep the best of both worlds. We extended the initially contracted period because we were extremely pleased with his early results and knew we needed his professional counsel as we continued to develop this new operational model." – Mike Hensen, Assistant Director of the Duke University Center on Globalization, Governance & Competitiveness

"If you are looking for a creative and strategic communicator to help achieve your individual and organizational goals, then I would highly recommend the services of Kevin Anselmo and Experiential Communications. Kevin is skilled at crafting compelling content and disseminating it to different audiences via traditional media and digital communications channels. His abilities in this area allowed College Advising Corps to expand its visibility nationally and effectively communicate key strategic messages to our different stakeholder groups." – Nicole Hurd, Founder and CEO of College Advising Corps

"Kevin Anselmo led a comprehensive review of our school's marketing and communications based on interviews and research. His support was invaluable in helping us gain clarity around what makes us unique and more importantly how to communicate it. We have followed a number of his recommendations as it relates to re-structuring our marketing

communications operations. Following the success of our initial project, we are continuing our collaboration so we can leverage Kevin's expertise and advice in executing an ongoing strategic marketing communications plan." – Danica Purg, President of IEDC Bled School of Management

"Kevin Anselmo is creative and client-centered in his approach to working with our team on communications, and we highly value the opportunity to partner with him. Kevin brings strong understanding and skills in content marketing and also in preparing professionals globally to leverage social media. He has been very flexible in working with our broader team and motivating engagement and alignment with the content strategy." – Christine Robers, Director of Global Marketing for Duke Corporate Education

Here are client testimonials about the value of our media training workshops:

"Whether you are considering Kevin's services for help with messaging strategy or for media training, I give him my highest possible recommendation. Kevin's work is consistently outstanding." – Bill Boulding, Dean of Duke University's Fuqua School of Business (former employer of Kevin Anselmo)

"The media training sessions provided by Experiential Communications were interactive, effective and highly enjoyable. Kevin has a polished but informal and approachable training style that worked really well for our team. We are already implementing many of the ready-to-use ideas we discussed and have set in motion several longer-term initiatives identified during the sessions." – David Young, CEO of VIF International

"Kevin Anselmo provided our faculty members with an all-day training workshop on the use of social media to advance their research efforts. Throughout the workshop he continually provided new insights on how these platforms can be used to expand one's impact and visibility. Some of our faculty are quite media savvy, but even the most knowledgeable were learning many new things from Kevin. He is very good at reading his audience and moving things along at the right pace to keep everyone

engaged. He was even able to provide a luddite such as myself with valuable takeaways that have proven very impactful!" – Joe Phillips, Dean of the Albers School of Business at Seattle University

"Kevin is an absolute professional. We invited him to speak at a training for a group of young social entrepreneurs. He provided helpful tips on how to effectively tailor a message to a variety of audiences, including the media, funders and the general public. He was very flexible and tailored his presentation to our specific group. I absolutely recommend working with Kevin and Experiential Communications!" – Maggie Woods, Fellow at the Institute for Emerging Issues at NC State University

NOTES

Introduction

Mark Farrell and John Davis on responding to higher education disruption. EFMD Global Focus Magazine, "Embrace Disruption", 2016. http://globalfocusmagazine.com/embrace-disruption/.

Question #1

Gallup State of the Workplace Report. Gallup website. June 11, 2013. http://www.gallup.com/businessjournal/162953/tackle-employees-stagnating-engagement.aspx.

University of Missouri Extension Message Map. University of Missouri Extension website. http://extension.missouri.edu/staff/marketing/messagemap/message_map8-10-04.pdf.

Question #2

Speaking French in your communications. "Spin Sucks - Communication and Reputation Management in the Digital Age" book by Gini Dietrich (Que Publishers). March 2014.

Question #3

David Meerman Scott. "Educate and inform instead of interrupt and sell." April 14, 2014. https://twitter.com/dmscott/status/455736493429239808

Marketing Magazine Canada: "About Us," Marketing Magazine Canada. http://www.marketingmag.ca/microsite/about/.

Stanford University's Graduate School of Business Publications: Stanford University Graduate School of Business website. https://www.gsb.stanford.edu/insights/about.

Question #4

Michael Hyatt eBooks. Michael Hyatt official website. https://michaelhyatt.com

Chris Ducker Launchpad. Chris Ducker official website. https://chrisducker.leadpages.co/youpreneur-launchpad-periscope/.

Social Media Marketing World. Social Media Examiner website. May 24, 2016. http://www.socialmediaexaminer.com/social-media-marketing-industry-report-2016/.

Question #5

Content Marketing Institute's email marketing. Content Marketing Institute website. http://info.contentmarketinginstitute.com/acton/form/5141/0022:d-0001/0/-/-/-/-/index.htm.

Interview with Handelsblatt. Duke Fuqua School of Business Europe Blog. October 17, 2016. https://regions.fuqua.duke.edu/europe/2016/10/17/veteran-news-editor-discusses-changes-in-german-economy?category=uncategorized.

Question #9

Edelman Trust Barometer. Edelman global communications marketing firm. January 2016. http://www.edelman.com/insights/intellectual-property/2016-edelman-trust-barometer/.

Question #10

Under New Management. David Burkus (Houghton Mifflin Harcourt Publishing). March 15, 2016. http://davidburkus.com/books/under-new-management/.

ABOUT THE AUTHOR

Kevin Anselmo is the Founder and Principal of Experiential Communications. He helps individuals and groups gain clarity about what to communicate. Once determined, he then works with his clients to disseminate those messages to ensure it is aligned to big-picture goals.

His services focus on communications strategy development, media training, PR execution, coaching, workshops and events, primarily for the higher education, research and entrepreneurial communities. His current and past clients include College Advising Corps; Duke Corporate Education; Duke University Center on Globalization, Governance & Competitiveness; Geneva Centre for Security Policy; IEDC Bled School of Management; IMD; Montreux School of Business; Nestle; North Carolina State University's Emerging Issues Initiative; North American Society for the Sociology of Sport; Seattle University; University of Tor Vergata in Rome; and VIF International Education.

Previously, Kevin was Director of Public Relations for Duke University's Fuqua School of Business and prior to that managed media relations for IMD in Switzerland. He lived and worked in Switzerland for eight years and in Germany for two years and has led public relations initiatives in various countries around the world. Currently, he resides in Chapel Hill, North Carolina with his wife and two young boys.

More information is at **www.experientialcommunications.com**. You can contact him at **kevin@experientialcommunications.com**.